D0926739

CLASSIC CARS
AN IMAGINATION LIBRARY SERIES

THE STORY OF THE

Ford
Mustang

by Jim Mezzanotte

GARETH STEVENS
GS
PUBLISHING
A WRC Media Company

Please visit our web site at: www.garethstevens.com
For a free color catalog describing Gareth Stevens Publishing's
list of high-quality books and multimedia programs,
call 1-800-542-2595 (USA) or 1-800-387-3178 (Canada).
Gareth Stevens Publishing's fax: (414) 332-3567.

Library of Congress Cataloging-in-Publication Data

Mezzanotte, Jim.
    The story of the Ford Mustang / by Jim Mezzanotte.
        p. cm. — (Classic cars: an imagination library series)
    Includes bibliographical references and index.
    ISBN 0-8368-4534-X (lib. bdg.)
    1. Mustang automobile—History—Juvenile literature. I. Title. II. Series.
TL215.M8M48   2005
629.222'2—dc22   2004059105

First published in 2005 by
Gareth Stevens Publishing
A WRC Media Company
330 West Olive Street, Suite 100
Milwaukee, WI 53212 USA

Text: Jim Mezzanotte
Cover design and page layout: Scott M. Krall
Series editors: JoAnn Early Macken and Mark J. Sachner
Picture Researcher: Diane Laska-Swanke

Photo credits: Cover, pp. 5, 7, 9, 13, 17, 19, 21 © Ron Kimball; p. 11 © National Motor Museum;
p. 15 © Javier Flores/Ron Kimball

Printed in the United States of America

1 2 3 4 5 6 7 8 9 09 08 07 06 05

Front cover: Ford Mustangs have been around for a long time. This Mustang is a 1964 model, the first year the cars were sold.

TABLE OF CONTENTS

Words that appear in the glossary are printed in **boldface** type the first time they occur in the text.

THE PONY CAR

In the early 1960s, Lee Iacocca had an idea. He worked at the Ford Motor Company. He thought Ford should make a car for young people. The car had to be small and sporty. It had to be inexpensive, too.

The **engineers** at Ford **designed** a new car. They named it the "Mustang." Mustangs are fast, wild ponies. Ford made a special Mustang for car shows. At these shows, people could see new car models. People loved the new Mustang! They called it the "pony car."

In the 1960s, most American cars were big. Lee Iacocca thought some Americans would like a smaller, sporty car, like this 1964 Mustang.

A SMASH HIT

Ford began selling Mustangs in 1964. They were a big success. Young people bought the cars. Older people bought them, too. Everybody loved the Mustang! Most American cars were big. The Mustang was small. It had a fresh new look. It reminded people of sports cars from Europe.

People could get different kinds of Mustangs. They could get a **coupe** or a **convertible**. They could get an engine with six **cylinders**. Or they could get a V-8 engine with eight cylinders. This engine was more powerful.

The Mustang broke sales records. In the first two years, Ford sold more than two million Mustangs!

When Mustangs came out, they were very popular. Many people bought Mustang convertibles, such as this model. They were fun to drive with the top down.

THE SHELBY MUSTANG

In 1965, a special Mustang came out. It was called the Shelby Mustang. Carroll Shelby made this car. Shelby was famous for the Shelby Cobra. He put a big Ford engine in a small British sports car. He called it the Cobra. It was very fast.

Ford sent Shelby some regular Mustangs. Shelby **modified** these Mustangs. He made them lighter and more powerful. He gave them special wheels and tires. The cars were like race cars. Some people did race them. The cars often won. Only a few Shelby Mustangs were made. Like the Cobra, they were fast!

It is easy to spot a Shelby Mustang. The cars have special wheels and racing stripes. This Mustang is a 1966 Shelby G.T. 350.

MUSCLE MANIA!

By the late 1960s, other companies were making sporty cars. Chevrolet made the Camaro. Plymouth made the Barracuda. Dodge made the Charger. These cars were called "muscle cars." They had big V-8 engines. The engines produced a lot of **horsepower**. They could **accelerate** very quickly.

The Mustang was the first muscle car. Ford wanted it to stay popular. The Mustang was given better brakes and **suspension**. It became wider. Then it could hold a larger engine. But Ford was not done yet. The race was on for more muscle!

By the late 1960s, Mustangs were bigger and faster. This Shelby Mustang is a 1968 model. It has a big V-8 engine.

THE BOSS

In 1970, Ford began selling the Boss 429. Some people think this car is the best Mustang ever made. It is the ultimate muscle car!

The heart of the Boss was its mighty engine. Ford designed this engine for racing. To use it in racing, Ford had to put it in regular cars. Ford put this engine in the Boss.

This engine was the largest Mustang engine ever. Ford had to modify the Mustang so the engine would fit. The engine had a huge amount of horsepower. No car had more muscle than the Boss!

This 1970 Boss 429 is a very fast car. The opening in the hood lets in air to its powerful engine.

RACING MUSTANGS

Mustangs won many races. Some Mustangs won at drag racing. In drag racing, two cars race in a straight line. They accelerate to a high speed. Some people used regular Mustangs. Other people used special Mustangs. The cars had powerful engines. They had bigger tires to grip the road.

Mustangs did well in Trans-Am races, too. In Trans-Am races, cars speed around racetracks with many twists and turns. People modified regular Mustangs for these races. The cars were very fast. They could go around corners quickly. In the 1960s, Mustangs raced other muscle cars. Mustangs won many Trans-Am races.

Mustangs have been very successful race cars. This 1970 Mustang was modified for Trans-Am racing.

NO MORE MUSCLE

In the early 1970s, Ford sold fewer Mustangs. Gas was more expensive. Many people bought smaller cars that used less gas. Mustangs used a lot of gas. Ford changed Mustang engines to cut down on **pollution**, but the engines were now less powerful.

People thought more about car safety. The government passed new laws to make cars safer. Many people worried about convertibles. They wondered what would happen if the cars rolled over. Ford stopped making Mustang convertibles.

In 1974, a new kind of Mustang came out. It was much smaller. The days of the big muscle cars were over.

This Mustang is a 1973 convertible. The 1974 model was a new, smaller kind of Mustang that only came with a hard top.

MODERN MUSTANGS

Ford kept improving the Mustang. A new model came out in 1979. It handled better. It had more power. It had a sharp-edged body. In 1983, Ford made a Mustang convertible. Some Mustangs had a **turbocharger** to boost power. Other Mustangs came with big V-8 engines. Fast Mustangs were back!

In the 1990s, a special Mustang came out. It was called the SVT Cobra. It had a new V-8 engine. A small team of workers built this engine. It was big and powerful. It barely fit in the car. The SVT Cobra was a very fast Mustang.

By the 1990s, Mustangs had become sleek, modern cars. But they were still fast and powerful. This Mustang is a 1995 Cobra.

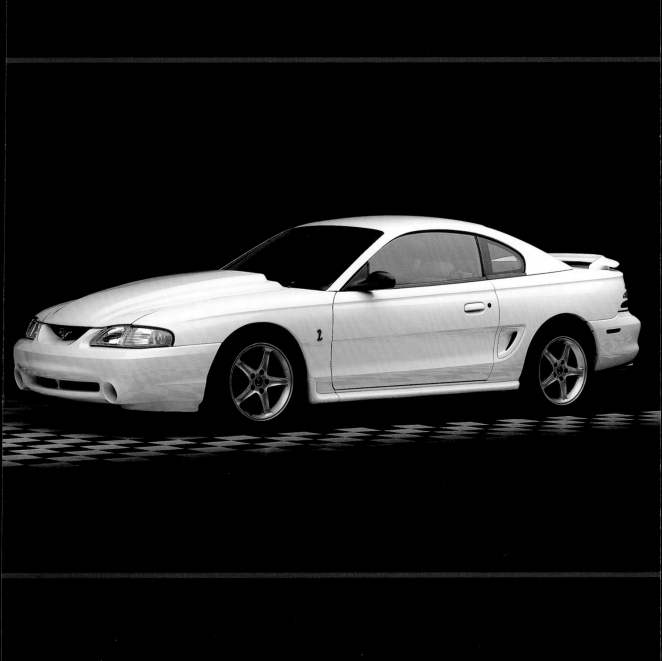

A PONY FOR TODAY

Ford still makes Mustangs. They have been around for forty years. Today, there is a new model. This car has many improvements. But it looks a lot like early Mustangs. The body has the same square shape. It has the same round headlights. The front **grille** looks similar, too.

The new model is sporty and exciting. It has a long hood to hold its big engine. It comes as a hard top or a convertible. It can have a V-8 engine. This engine is light but powerful. The new Mustang is fast. It is fun to drive. The pony car is still popular!

This 2005 Mustang looks similar to Mustangs from the 1960s. Like those cars, it has a pony on the grill, and it is fun to drive.

MORE TO READ AND VIEW

Books (Nonfiction)   *Classic American Cars.* Quentin Willson (DK Publishing)
Muscle Cars. Roaring Rides (series). Tracy Maurer (Rourke Publishing)
Mustang. Ultimate Cars (series). A. T. McKenna (Abdo & Daughters
Publishing)
Mustangs. Great American Muscle Cars (series). Eric Ethan (Gareth
Stevens Publishing)

Videos (Nonfiction)   *America's Favorite Cars: The Complete Mustang.* (Red Distribution)
Ford Mustang. (White Star)
How a Car Is Built. (Think Media)
The Visual History of Cars: Mustang (MPI Home Video)

PLACES TO WRITE AND VISIT

Here are three places to contact for more information:

Mustang Club of America
4051 Barrancas Ave, PMB 102
Pensacola, FL 32507
USA
1-850-438-0626
www.mustang.org

Peterson Automotive Museum
6060 Wilshire Blvd.
Los Angeles, CA 90036
USA
1-323-930-2277
www.peterson.org

Shelby American Collection
5020 Chaparral Court
P.O. Box 19228
Boulder, CO 80308
USA
1-303-516-9565
**www.shelbyamerican
collection.org**

WEB SITES

Web sites change frequently, but we believe the following web sites are going to last. You can also use good search engines, such as **Yahooligans!** [www.yahooligans.com] or **Google** [www.google.com], to find more information about Ford Mustang. Here are some keywords to help you: *Boss 429, Carroll Shelby, Ford, GT350, muscle car, Mustang, pony car,* and *SVT Cobra.*

popularmechanics.com/
automotive/sub_coll_vintage/
1998/6/67_shelby_mustang/
This web site from *Popular Mechanics* magazine is all about a 1967 Shelby Mustang. It has pictures of the car, including views of the engine and interior.

www.allfordmustangs.com/Detailed/
2208.shtml
Visit this web page to see a special 2003 Mustang. It has been modified for racing. The site has information about the car and many pictures, too.

www.allfordmustangs.com/forums/photo
post/showgallery.php/cat/3233/password/
Visit this web page for pictures of many Mustangs, including racing Mustangs.

www.classiccar.com/photopost/
showgallery.php?cat=517&password=
This site has a photo gallery of Mustang engines and interiors.

www.fordvehicles.com/2005mustang/
home.asp
At this official Ford web site, you can find information about the latest Mustang and see pictures of the inside and outside of the car.

www.nvsaac.com/gallery/1966_main.htm
This web site has pictures of many different Shelby Mustangs.

www.ritzsite.net/Shelby-Mustang/
01_Shelby-Mustang.htm
Visit this site for a history of Shelby Mustangs and many pictures of the cars.

www.vintage-mustang.com/show02.html
At the web site, you can see pictures from a Mustang car show. The site has pictures of many different Mustangs built in the 1960s.

GLOSSARY

You can find these words on the pages listed. Reading a word in a sentence helps you understand it even better.

accelerate (ack-SELL-ur-ate) — increase speed. 10, 14

convertible (kun-VER-tuh-bull) — a car with a top that can be folded down or removed. 6, 16, 18, 20

coupe (KOOP) — a car with a hard top and two doors. 6

cylinders (SIL-in-durz) — tubes inside an engine where gas explodes, giving the engine power. 6

designed (dee-ZINED) — made the plans for something. 4, 12

engineers (en-jun-EARZ) — people who design machines. 4

grille (GRYL) — the opening in a car that lets in air to cool the engine. 20

horsepower (HORS-pow-ur) — the amount of power an engine makes, based on how much work one horse can do. 10, 12

modified (MOD-if-eyed) — made changes to something. 8, 12, 14

pollution (puh-LOO-shun) — man-made waste that harms people and the environment. 16

suspension (suh-SPEN-shun) — the parts that connect the wheels to a car and help the car go smoothly over bumps. 10

turbocharger (TUR-boe-char-jur) — something that forces more air into an engine, giving it more power. 18

INDEX